JAN 08 2020

Equal Access
Fighting for Disability Protections™

Networking for Teens with Disabilities and Their Allies

Marcela D. Grillo

Rosen
YA™

New York

Published in 2020 by The Rosen Publishing Group, Inc.
29 East 21st Street, New York, NY 10010

Library of Congress Cataloging-in-Publication Data

Names: Grillo, Marcela D., author.
Title: Networking for teens with disabilities and their allies / Marcela D. Grillo.
Description: New York: Rosen Publishing, 2020 | Series: Equal access: Fighting for disability protections | Includes bibliographical references and index. | Audience: Grades 7–12.
Identifiers: LCCN 2018013428| ISBN 9781508183822 (library bound) | ISBN 9781508185925 (pbk.)
Subjects: LCSH: Teenagers with disabilities—Juvenile literature. | Social media—Juvenile literature. | Online social networks—Juvenile literature.
Classification: LCC HV1569.3.Y68 G75 2019 | DDC 302.23/1087—dc23
LC record available at https://lccn.loc.gov/2018013428

Manufactured in the United States of America

The editors of this resource have consulted various organizations' style guides, including that of the National Center on Disability and Journalism, to ensure the language herein is accurate, sensitive, and respectful. In accordance with NCDJ's recommendation, we have deferred to our author's preference of either people-first or identity-first language.

For some of the images in this book, the people photographed are models and the depictions do not imply actual situations or events.

Table of Contents

Introduction

According to the 2016 Disability Statistics Annual Report by the Center on Disability at the Public Health Institute, 7.2 percent of the US population with disabilities were youth and adolescents, ages five to seventeen. These disabilities can be physical, such as hearing loss or visual impairment, or so-called "invisible" disabilities, such as autism, diabetes, or bipolar disorder. These disabilities can also range in severity, or the level in which it has impacted the person.

Being a teenager with a disability comes with its own set of victories and struggles. Living with a disability might make teenagers feel insecure and could even negatively impact how they feel about their own bodies, if the disability is physical. According to the Center on Disability's 2016 Disability Statistics Annual Report, 5.4 percent of youth between the ages of five and seventeen have a disability. To break it down by type in 2015, 0.6 percent of youth between the ages of five and seventeen had a hearing disability; 0.8 percent had a vision disability; 4.1 percent had a cognitive disability; and 0.6 percent had an ambulatory disability.

Even though obstacles exist, there are still ways for disabled teens to thrive socially and emotionally through creating lasting, fulfilling friendships. Getting to know someone with a disability who has faced similar struggles and

Guide dogs allow people who are visually impaired to remain independent by helping them navigate through any physical obstacles they encounter in their daily routines.

triumphs can build confidence while fighting off loneliness and isolation.

These friendships can be seen as a way to network as well as have fun. A network is just a fancy way of saying a group of people who are organized for a shared purpose. Not only can you form a network among friends or classmates and peers—a social network—but there are also professional networks among adults in the working

Disabled people can thrive at work as long as they have the proper accommodations and a strong network of colleagues. It's never too early for teens to start making connections that will help them when they enter the workforce.

world, a community that disabled teens will join in the future when they are searching for jobs. Therefore, networking can be seen as a worthwhile business tool, too. Other types of networks can be initiated through social media, utilizing popular platforms like Facebook or Instagram. Additionally, networks can be formed through a teen's health care team, which provides assistance with managing a disability or medical condition.

Chapter One

Building a Network Through Friendship

Creating and keeping friendships is the foundation of a network: through maintaining relationships with other people. Your friend network is extremely important, as it may be able to help all of you get through tough times.

The manual *Friends, Connecting People with Disabilities and Community Members* by Angela Amado focuses on encouraging those who are disabled to forge relationships with community members, generally those who are not disabled. As a helpful tactic, Amado writes about making a relationship map, which is just a visual representation of one's connections to the community. This can be useful for both disabled teens and their nondisabled allies, so that they can be aware of whom they are including, and excluding, from their network.

Amado outlines four steps to making this relationship map:

- The person making the map puts herself in the middle.
- The first, innermost circle is for the people she sees and interacts with most often.
- In the next circle, she puts the people she knows

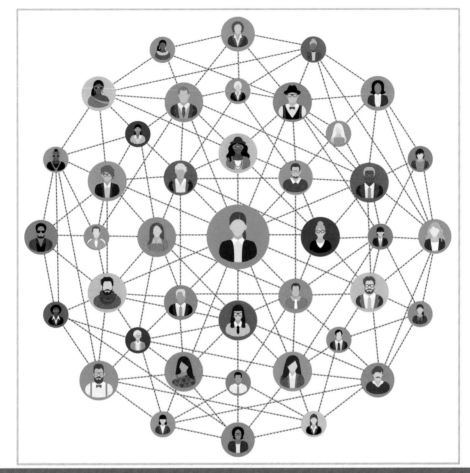

Relationship maps help people visualize who is part of their network. The subject puts herself in the middle of the map and widens out to include both people she is close to and acquaintances.

but not as well as those in the first circle.
- The outermost circle is for acquaintances, people she may know by name but is not close to.

Building sustainable friendships between those who are disabled and those who are not takes a "different type of effort," according to Amado. She outlines several strategies one can use to nurture these friendships. One strategy is talking about shared interests and respective talents. For example, a teen may be intrigued by the idea of learning to play an instrument, and he befriends someone who is skilled at playing the guitar. They can bond over this interest and even learn from one another. This type of friendship would be mutually beneficial, meaning it can be a positive situation for both people.

Unfortunately—and unfairly—there can be a stigma surrounding disabled people, which can affect friendships and other relationships. If non-disabled teens have negative beliefs about their disabled peers, viewing them as different or less than, it will take work to overcome that bias.

However, just because those with disabilities are stigmatized does not mean that friendships can't

Connecting over a shared interest is a fantastic way to make friends and network. Whether you're involved with music, sports, or activism, these common bonds will help you form strong relationships.

blossom in the face of it. In the article "Fostering Friendship: Supporting Relationships Among Youth with and without Developmental Disabilities" authors Erik Carter, Jennifer Asmus, and Colleen Moss state that there are ways to facilitate friendships between disabled and nondisabled adolescents. These include having more inclusive classrooms so that disabled and nondisabled students have a chance to interact on a daily basis. These interactions can also extend to noninstructional settings, such after-school activities or lunchtime in the cafeteria. The authors also suggest educating nondisabled students about their peers' disabilities and having support personnel, such as aides or paraprofessionals, intervene less often to allow the space for friendships to blossom.

Another important part of friendship, particularly between disabled and nondisabled teenagers, is something many experts call "coming out as disabled," or a teen revealing or discussing his disability to and with others. There are many ways one can do this; one way is sharing experiences of living with a

Talking honestly about some of the struggles that come with being disabled can bring you closer to your nondisabled friends and classmates.

disability with classmates and friends. These experiences can be times of success or times of struggle.

Camp SMILE

United Cerebral Palsy (UCP)'s Camp SMILE is a recreational summer camp that serves individuals ages five to fifty with different kinds of disabilities,

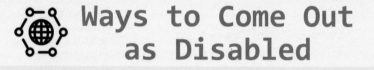

Ways to Come Out as Disabled

- Participate in different kinds of disability activism. Activism is all about taking a stance for what one believes in. For example, one may join the fight for social equality.
- Raise awareness to bring about change. Sharing what it's like to live with a disability can start a vital conversation between disabled teens and those who are not disabled and don't understand what daily life is like for their disabled peers.
- Use social media. Blogging is an excellent, personal way to discuss one's experiences of living with a disability.
- Take part in fun activities aimed toward youth and teenagers with disabilities.

ranging from but not limited to: cerebral palsy, autism, muscular dystrophy, Down syndrome, and traumatic brain injury. Some of the activities Camp SMILE offers are swimming, boating, fishing, arts and crafts, horseback riding, zip lines, and archery. Camp SMILE has adaptive equipment so that their campers can fully participate and have fun. Beginning new friendships through common interests and shared activities such as the ones offered at Camp SMILE is a fantastic way to network with other teenagers with disabilities and allies, too. A shared passion for the outdoors, for example, is a great place to start getting to know each other better.

Sharing disability experiences with new people can be scary and nerve-wracking, but there is comfort in knowing others may relate to those experiences. There should be an element of acceptance and kindness in sharing with another person. You don't have to associate only with those who have the same type of disability.

There is an unspoken understanding that goes across the disability spectrum: those who are disabled know what it's like to live with a disability. However, that does not mean that disabled teens can only, or should only, make friends with other disabled teens. Friendships between disabled and nondisabled teens are not only very possible, but also encouraged. A disabled teen sharing her experiences with a nondisabled friend can widen her friend's understanding of what living with a disability is really like. The nondisabled teen can then appreciate what the disabled teen goes through and even learn something new along the way.

Myths & Facts

Myth: If I tell my friends about my disability, they'll respect me less.

Fact: Discussing one's disability broadens and deepens friendships and often educates nondisabled friends. True friends embrace the person, disability and all.

Myth: As a disabled youth, I can have only friends who have disabilities.

Fact: Friendships between disabled and non-disabled teens can be extremely rewarding and help break down stereotypes of what it means to have a disability.

Myth: Having a disability makes it harder for me to make real friends.

Fact: Having a disability can be a positive in this situation, because then one wouldn't make friends with anyone who is judgmental and ignorant.

Chapter Two

What Is an Ally?

In the most basic terms, an allyship can be defined as a relationship in which both people support one another and help one another in times of need. Being an ally comes with the responsibility to learn and be open-minded about what it means to be friends with someone with a disability and to accept that their experiences differ from one's own.

A blog post written by Anna Corbitt on the website Paraquad: The Disability Experts (www .paraquad.org) outlines effective ways for the non-disabled to be allies to those who are disabled, for instance by asking what words the teen with a disability would prefer or feel comfortable with. This gives the teen a sense of control, while also making sure there is no tension between the two people because they are worrying about what to say and what language to use.

Being an Ally Versus Being a Friend

Being a friend and being an ally can very well mean the same thing. An ally can be someone a disabled teen can relate to; someone with empathy for issues that affect the disabled community. This bond can be established through sharing common interests, such as fighting for social justice. Though a nondisabled ally may not know exactly what his disabled companion has gone through, he can definitely be sympathetic to the cause if, for example, he is interested in disability activism. Perhaps this nondisabled ally has a brother, sister, or parent who is disabled. This nondisabled ally would understand what the disabled person is going through,

Activists protest in New York City to highlight the need for accessible subway stations. By supporting causes they believe in, disabled teens can be part of a community that fights for the rights of disabled people.

even though she might not share the exact experience. Understanding and personal connections are extremely important, as they can inspire the ally to be all the more involved in the cause.

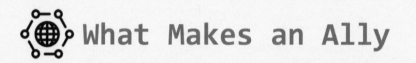 **What Makes an Ally**

A great ally:

- Is informed about his friend's particular disability. Being informed demonstrates a genuine interest or concern about what a disabled friend may be going through. It shows the teen with a disability that his disability matters and that all parts of his identity are valued and appreciated. He is valued for all that he is.
- Doesn't always make the disability or medical condition the main focus. Teenagers with disabilities are so much more than their diagnoses. They are well-rounded human beings, with so many great qualities to offer the world. An ally should recognize and encourage all of a friend's qualities.
- Asks educated questions—and doesn't assume! Asking questions gets the conversation going and keeps everyone informed in a positive way. Curiosity is a wonderful attribute, but making assumptions could lead to confusion and hurt feelings.

Making Friends

Making friends is an important part of growing up. Sometimes youth and teens with disabilities have a harder time making friends than their nondisabled peers. According to a study about friendship for youth and teens with disabilities called "The Goal of Making Friends for Youth with Disabilities,", there are four common themes when it comes to making friends.

The first theme involved communication, social skills, and interests.

The second theme was how much the youth interviewed for the study prioritized making friends. According to this study, the youth's parents also supported their child's desire to develop friendships.

The third theme was about the chances, or opportunities, the participants had to actually make friends. According to the study's research, some of the opportunities that could help begin

It can be difficult for disabled teens to make friends, leading to feelings of isolation. But joining a club or therapy group offers teens a chance to form close connections with their peers.

friendships were clubs, extracurricular activities, therapy groups, and school-based activities.

The fourth theme involved was about a disabled teen's motivation to make friends. For example, youth with disabilities have to want to keep their friends and shouldn't rely on their parents to do it for them.

The study explored the relationships between these themes and also created what is called a goal menu specifically for friend making. These menus can help youth, parents, and their health care providers identify goals when it comes to making friends, like whether or not the youth have joined an extracurricular activity run by their school. They wanted to create a guide for making friends.

Tips for Making Friends

- Get out there: Try to attend an activity hosted in your local community. At these activities, one may find someone with shared interests, and the friendship can develop from there.
- Start the conversation: Going up to someone new and trying to start a conversation can be frightening at first, but the rewards can be great. You never know who your next friend will be. Try sitting next to someone new in the cafeteria or during class.

(continued on the next page)

(continued from the previous page)

- Be yourself: Don't change who you are to try to make friends. The qualities that make you unique are exactly what will make others want to get to know you.

A fun creative endeavor like an arts and crafts class gives disabled teens an opportunity to pursue a favorite hobby while forming meaningful friendships.

Sometimes it might be hard to keep friendships because a teen with a physical disability is not able to take part in activities in places that are not accessible. However, if the teen were the one to suggest an activity, like going to the movies or out to lunch, she could make sure the place was accessible for her. It's good to take initiative with one's friends because it helps keep the friendship fresh.

Different Kinds of Allies

An ally can come in many different forms, whether it be a parent, sibling, or even a health care provider. A parent can help advocate for his or her disabled teen, offer advice, or just be there to listen to his or her child talk through a problem he is having. A sibling can perform the same role, as can a health care provider, which could be a doctor, nurse, or therapist. A certain level of trust develops between a provider and patient, a connection that goes beyond the role that the person plays in the teen's medical or psychiatric care.

Even if the health care provider is not disabled, he or she is familiar with the problems that relate to being disabled and likely has a wealth of information to share. Because of this experience, he

A disabled teen's health care providers can be excellent allies and a vital part of her network. Experienced medical professionals are a great source of information and support.

or she will show compassion for the patient's concerns and have the patience to talk things through. Whether a teen has a visible or invisible disability, there is always an emotional component to the condition. Emotions can affect one's overall well-being, too. Being healthy has a great deal to do with both wellness and mental health.

Wellness can be approached and defined in many different ways, but the National Wellness Institute (https://www.nationalwellness.org) states that, among other things, wellness is "a conscious, self-directed, and evolving process of achieving full potential." Wellness is multidimensional, incorporating not only the person's mental and spiritual health, as well as his deep connection to the environment. In addition, wellness is holistic, or heavily interconnected, and is better referred to as a whole entity rather than parts. Above all, the institute considers wellness to be a "positive and affirming" concept. Working with family and providers, disabled teens can use the principles of wellness to create a fuller and richer life.

Chapter Three

Using Social Media

Another great way to network would be through the use of a social media platform, such as Facebook, which has 1.8 billion monthly users. Although being active on social media comes with risks, it can greatly enrich the lives of disabled teens. Facebook in particular offers many ways for the disabled community to share both support and resources.

Finding Friends

There are many groups on Facebook that allow you to communicate exclusively with others who also have a disability. This communication can then become a form of support for those with disabilities. With so many Facebook users, there are ample opportunities to connect with teens who have similar interests and concerns.

Joining a Facebook group also allows users to trade information that can help them overcome obstacles that stem from their disabilities or differences. A teen with a physical disability might join a group to ask for advice on a city's most accessible

Social networking sites like Facebook can be a great place for disabled teens around the world to share their stories and get both emotional and practical support.

restaurants or to look for accessible places to hang out and have fun with friends or family. Being part of a Facebook group also allows you to connect with users who live far away, which can be particularly helpful for those who are physically disabled. Expanding a friendship circle opens up a world of possibilities to teens searching for community as well as coping skills.

For teens with a hearing impairment, Facebook can be a useful platform because most of the site's features do not need audio in order to be beneficial. A report by Media Access Australia offers tips and tricks about how to overcome the accessibility issues that exist on Facebook, particularly for those who are blind or vision impaired. One suggestion is to use the mobile app, which some consider more user friendly for those with disabilities.

Everyone using Facebook must be cautious. So-called data mining companies have obtained the information of millions of users without their permission. While deleting your Facebook account is one option, you have to weigh the risks and benefits of using the platform.

Facebook groups aimed at the disabled can provide information about many topics, such as which restaurants in a particular city are most accessible.

When posting photographs to Facebook or another social media site, it's wise to ask others who are in the photo if it's okay to put it up on the platform. Also, don't overshare on the internet by putting something of an extremely personal nature out there, as that may make you more likely to be taken advantage of. What is on the internet is permanent, so think about the possible repercussions before posting on your timeline.

When using Facebook, there are several ways to monitor what one posts or comments on, in addition to what one sees. For example, if a user sets a status or photograph to public, it can be seen by those who are not on your friends list if someone clicks the Like button or comments on the picture.

Use caution when commenting or posting on public pages as well because those posts and comments will show up on news feeds and can go viral, leading to potential embarrassment or worse.

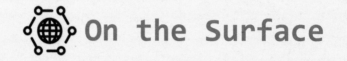 On the Surface

- There are times when using social media can be emotionally draining. Because many people typically post their highlights instead of their struggles, it's easy to feel like everyone else is having more fun and have fewer problems in their lives, especially when you are struggling with a disability. But just because someone is showcasing her favorite moments doesn't mean she never feels lonely, overwhelmed, or exhausted. It's important to feel good about yourself and have a positive attitude even if your life doesn't seem as perfect on the surface. Remember, social media is often more about presentation than truth.
- It's easy to become too attached, or even addicted, to social media. Spending much of your time on social media may begin to replace face-to-face interaction with those you care about or want to know better. Excessive texting can have the same effect. Guard against losing touch with loved ones by prioritizing those relationships. These connections are healthy and beneficial. Too much screen time is not.

Staying Safe While Using Facebook

Just as using Facebook comes with benefits, it also comes with potential risks: communicating with people one doesn't know, for example, can be dangerous. Do not accept or trade messages with strangers. If a stranger tries to reach out, do not respond. He may be looking to exploit, bully, or even abuse you, especially if he believes that a dis- ability makes a teen more vulnerable to a stranger's tactics. If a stranger reaches out and uses crude or offensive language, report this offense to Facebook.

An important feature on Facebook allows teens to block a user from seeing all her posts and pho- tographs. As for sharing photographs, one should only share photographs of people, places, or things she wants her Facebook friends to see. Never post personal or sensitive information on your newsfeed, like your home address or telephone number.

A teenager on social media should also be aware of the potential exposure to inappropriate content. Get Safe Online (https://www.getsafeonline .org), a website devoted to online safety, explains this possible exposure as: "being able to access … sexually explicit, racist, violent, extrem- ist …" subject matter, whether by design or in error. In addition, many social media sites have a live-streaming feature, which allows users to post incidents of violence, bullying, or other harmful acts as they are actually happening.

Cyberbullying

Cyberbullying is a serious issue in today's society among our youth. Through networking on social media, one might receive threatening, hurtful, or harmful messages of an intimidating nature. It's important to recognize the signs that a disabled person is being bullied. According to the website StopBullying.gov (www .stopbullying.gov), 92 percent of teens between the ages of thirteen and seventeen are online daily. One out of ten boys and one out of five girls are cyberbullied. Some warning signs include using their phones or other electronic devices less often, hiding their screens or devices when around others, shutting down one account just to open another, avoiding social interactions, and becoming depressed or anxious.

It is crucial to know how to defend against cyberbullying. Parents, guardians, or other trusted adults should take

Bullying is extremely harmful and can take many forms, including gossiping about a classmate. When a disabled teen is excluded or mocked, he can become depressed.

a similar approach to address cyberbullying as they would face-to-face bullying: support the disabled teen who is going through this ordeal, and make it clear that you take his or her concerns seriously. If a parent suspects that his or her teen is being cyberbullied, take note of his or her behavior and have a frank and supportive conversation. Ask for details: how did the cyberbullying start and who was involved? What are the specifics of the cyberbullying? Another crucial step would be to document all instances of cyberbullying, and take screenshots of the bullying behavior, if possible. If the bullies are classmates, report them to the school. Facebook and other social media sites, like Twitter, can be contacted directly to have offensive or hurtful material removed. And depending on the severity of the bullying, law enforcement may have to become involved.

Taking a Turn on Twitter

People who use Twitter are drawn to the platform because of its fast, personal communication. Those who tweet really want to share their thoughts with others, whether it be a personal anecdote, an opinion about something they saw on cable news, or the latest bit of celebrity gossip. For those with disabilities, Twitter can be a wonderful way to look for relevant information on how to deal with disability-related issues, and, like Facebook, provide support for disabled teens as they find others with a common experience.

Using Social Media to Raise Awareness

- Take advantage of social media's influence: social media greatly increases the possibility of connecting with others. Because social media is used by millions of people, there is a good chance that with the right promotion, one's personal story of experiences with disability activism could reach a wide audience and raise awareness of issues surrounding the disability.
- Take advantage of having many of your contacts on social media. You can make friends, allies, and professional contacts throughout the country and around the globe. Connecting digitally not only makes networking easier and more efficient, but could also expand one's network by introducing different people with similar visions and passions.

Video chatting is one way to keep your network close, which can be great for friendships and for raising awareness about issues important to disabled teens.

As with Facebook, Twitter's developers have been criticized for its inaccessible features. Some of these issues have to do with the site's layout and font-size limitations. A surefire way to reach a broader audience—specifically, those with disabilities—is to join in on disability-related discussions by using the hashtags #a11y as well as #disability. Using these hashtags connects disabled teens to information about various disabilities, as well as how to be a successful ally. With the help of Twitter, teens get connected to organizations that advocate for the disabled, a practical, modern example of networking. Use the same caution with Twitter that you use with Facebook to keep yourself safe.

The Power of Instagram

Another way to utilize social media as a networking tool is via Instagram. Instagram is photo and video based, and what's useful is that users can link their Facebook, Twitter, and Flickr accounts to their Instagram accounts. According to Instagram, there are about four hundred million users worldwide. Many use Instagram because of its emphasis on photographs and videos, though it is very similar to Facebook in other ways.

As with other platforms, Instagram also has accessibility issues. According to Media Access Australia, because of "the lack of users providing alternative text, caption support and audio description, vision and hearing-impaired users may face challenges in using Instagram." One way to overcome these challenges would be to add alternative text as well as a text transcript to make it more accessible to the visually impaired.

Blogging as Someone with a Disability

Another useful way to use social media to network is through blogging. Blogging is all about one's own personal and creative expression. Those who blog usually want to communicate their thoughts and feelings to others online. Blogging can be about these general feelings, or it can be centered on a specific topic or issue that is deemed important to the blogger: these topics and issues can be political in nature or cover social or cultural happenings.

Because of its personal and intimate feel, blogging can be a fantastic platform for those with disabilities to share musings or ponder and reflect on disability-related issues. A blogger might want to write about how his experiences living with a disability fits—or does not fit—into society's views on what it means to have a disability. Blogging could also raise awareness on living with a disability and advocate for a cause that helps those with disabilities. The possibilities are endless.

Chapter Four

Different Ways to Network

There are many ways to network and meet others, whether at events, through mutual friends, or on social media. You can find potential friends at events centered on a common interest, like a book club or different kinds of meet-ups. These sorts of clubs can be sponsored by a community group or neighborhood public spaces, like a library. Another type of meeting could be geared toward teens with disabilities and center around how to live healthy, fulfilling lives. NYU Langone Hospital, in New York City, has an Initiative for Women with Disabilities (IWD), a center that works to meet the unique emotional and physical needs of women and adolescent girls who live with physical disabilities. In addition to providing primary and gynecological care, the IWD hosts programs, workshops, and classes. Some of these classes include tai chi, arthritis exercise, and mat Pilates, as well as chair yoga. This is a wonderful way to meet other girls and women who also have physical disabilities, which in turn is a way to expand one's network.

Participating in an exercise class, such as yoga, helps disabled teens stay physically and mentally fit while expanding their social circle.

Changing the Image

The website Diversability (www.diversability.org) strives to change the image of disability through the power of one's own community. An entry by clinical psychologist Dr. Danielle Sheypuk on the site focused on Girl Fuse, which is about "providing a platform for teen girls with physical disabilities from all over the world to unite and share their stories with each other and with everyone else."

According to Sheypuk, this sharing of stories is a great way to network and meet new people, diminish negative stereotypes, become empowered, and, moreover, add a powerful force to the disability rights movement. Girl Fuse is a project of Teen Voices, an initiative of Women's eNews, which boasts personal stories and news stories by and about girls with disabilities.

Get Out There (GOT) is an organization in the United Kingdom that assists young people in accessing fun leisure activities. One thirteen-year-old teen has taken to the stage to portray the deaf and blind activist Helen Keller. GOT built up her confidence and let her do things like go to the movies with her friends and go on vacation to Italy, building up her network of friends and allies along

In this photo, a student at a theater camp in Omaha, Nebraska, practices a dance routine. The camp, run by the Munroe-Meyer Institute, offers programs for people with developmental disabilities.

the way. The need for this web of connection is truly universal.

Networking Through an Organization

Disability Allies (www.disabilityallies.com) is a New Jersey-based nonprofit organization that strives to connect young adults and teens with disabilities with those who are nondisabled. Disability Allies hosts different events at which mentors and mentees mingle, with the mentors providing guidance and support while ensuring safe and encouraging environments. The mentees attend events with the goal of becoming more comfortable in social situations and creating lasting friendships. One mentee is paired with one mentor at the event, but the hope is that the friendship goes beyond the first meeting. Some past events that Disability Allies have hosted include a kickball event, a dance party, a barbecue in the park, and a transition to college day, at which college students were paired with high school students with disabilities to talk about the transition from high school to college. The beauty is the friendships formed between two people with different experiences, and this can happen no matter where you live.

Disability Allies also offers coaching services to those with disabilities, which include job coaching, volunteer coaching, social coaching and community integration, college or trade school assistance and preparation, and life skills. The job coaching helps teens and young adults with disabilities create résumés and find job opportunities. This is a great example of building one's own network that is based both in the community and in the professional sphere.

Disability Allies provides wonderful volunteer opportunities, at which one can not only volunteer directly with the organization, but also around their neighborhood. The organization promotes community inclusion and helps disabled teens find different clubs or interest groups and events, those centered around photography or hiking, for instance. Coaching includes life skills, which can have to do with anything from computer skills, like using Microsoft Word or Excel, to independent living skills, like preparing meals, cleaning and doing chores, and grocery shopping and paying bills, to name a few.

Online Dating

Another way for teens with disabilities to connect with the wider world is through online dating. In "For Teens with Disabilities, Flirting Can Be Easier Online," an article on the Women's eNews website, author Maggie Freleng states that teens who are physically disabled might be less likely to date because of their difficulty walking and navigating public spaces. In addition, it might be difficult to find a place for the date that is accessible. According to Dr. Danielle Sheypuk, joining an online dating site can be a great way for disabled teens to start socializing and putting oneself out there as someone interested in a romantic relationship. If disabled teens are not able to socialize in the same way as their nondisabled peers, they may feel lonely, isolated, and left behind when it comes to the dating scene, missing out on milestones like a first kiss.

Although sites like OKCupid (www.okcupid.com) and Match.com dominate the online dating scene, you must be at least eighteen years old to use the service. There are other sites geared more toward teens. Skout is an online flirting service aimed at people who are a minimum of thirteen years old and has several features that make it easier for users to connect with people who are in their age range. For example, Skout has two communities: one meant for adults and one meant for teens. The teen community is grouped by school grade to make sure the whole experience is age appropriate. The creators of Skout are also very serious about keeping their communities safe and monitor them regularly.

Dating can be complicated for disabled people, but also very rewarding. Having fun is a priority, but it's also important to stay safe.

In "Dating with a Disability," an article in the *New York Times*, author Wendy Lu details the experiences of multiple women with muscular dystrophy and other disabilities. The article addresses the women's desire to date and be seen as potential wives and mothers by men they are interested in getting to know. However, because of misconceptions about those who are disabled, this desire does not always come to pass. Dating can be tumultuous for everyone, disabled and nondisabled alike, but it can be particularly difficult for whose disabilities are seen as limiting. According to Lu, women who have physical disabilities begin to date much later in life. This is disheartening because disabled young women want to enjoy the same aspects of dating that nondisabled young women do, like meeting new people at a dance club or crowded café.

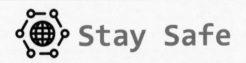 Stay Safe

When getting together with someone you met online, make sure to follow these guidelines:

- Always meet in a public place. Never agree to a date or to meet up at the person's home or somewhere too far away. It is always better to meet in a location that is familiar.

(continued on the next page)

(continued from the previous page)

- Tell a friend or family member where the date will be. This way, if the situation is uncomfortable, this friend or family member will know where you are.
- Keep the first date to under an hour. Although the two of you have developed an online relationship, when meeting face to face for the first time, it's best to take things slow.
- Don't get into someone's car. If he offers you a ride home, politely decline. It may feel awkward, but your safety comes first.

A disabled teen can certainly date someone with the same, or a different, disability. She can also date a nondisabled individual. She may find someone who is accepting, open minded, and available as a potential partner. Online dating can also allow for two people to begin a relationship in a less formal, low-pressure environment. Participating in an online forum can also help disabled teenagers work on their social skills, such as becoming better at flirting or even less shy, if shyness is an obstacle. Disabled teens are intrigued by dating, relationships, and intimacy, just like those who are not disabled, although those with disabilities are unfortunately often left out of the conversation and left on the sidelines of the dating world.

In online dating scenarios, people who are nondisabled may read a profile that mentions a disability and think that the person is more severely

Setting Up a Great Dating Profile

A successful dating profile should include the following:

- An effective description: Center your profile around the aspects of your personality that make you unique and someone whom others might like to know. Mention interests, hobbies, and passions. Keep the profile short and intriguing.
- Photos: Post appropriate, tasteful photographs that highlight your personality. If you love to play a particular sport, show yourself in that setting. Or if traveling is a passion, use a photo from a recent trip or excursion.
- Mentioning the disability: Disabled teens who use online dating sites may have different views on whether to put their disabilities on their profiles. Some may not want to lead with it, while others may believe that they have nothing to hide and that the person they are interested in should know everything up front. If you decide not to disclose that you are disabled at the start, think about the repercussions of keeping that information to yourself.

disabled than he actually is. This might stem from the nondisabled teen's preconception of what disability means, whether based on her own experiences or things she saw on television or in the movies. This may lead her to choose not to get to know a young adult with a disability. A disabled teen may decide to initially conceal the fact that he is disabled. However, there is the potential that this decision could backfire once the disability is revealed. It is understandable to not want to be defined by your disability. But disability is part of who you are, and when someone gets to know you that person will discover that you are so much more than your illness or condition.

Putting one's disability on a profile is also a way to filter out those who are worth getting to know. Of course, this does not guarantee that everyone who contacts you on a dating site will have read the entire profile. That's why it's important to keep the profile brief, purposeful, and intriguing. A good tactic is to double-check with the person you are messaging that he or she is indeed aware of the disability and OK with pursuing a relationship. If the answer is yes, the conversation can continue, and if the answer is no, then you can end things right there. Having a disability should not stop someone from being valued and desired. Everyone, disabled and nondisabled, deserves to experience deep connection with another person.

Just as using social media comes with risks, so does online dating. Online dating comes with a greater possibility of receiving unwanted or inappropriate messages and images, as well as sexual propositions from strangers. If said messages are explicit and make a user uncomfortable, those messages should immediately be reported to the people who run the dating site.

Networking Using LinkedIn

Besides using social media platforms to make friends and initiate romantic relationships, one can use those platforms as a helpful business tool. LinkedIn is a popular social networking site that is centered on making professional connections related to employment. Users can create personal résumés that list the work experience, education, and credentials that would make them suitable for a certain job. Users can also build a digital network of professional contacts, contribute to different work-related discussions, and follow organizations that pique the users' interests.

LinkedIn can be useful in connecting job seekers to possible employers, as well as allowing users to stay in touch with those

Being active on LinkedIn is a powerful way to develop a professional network. You can post a résumé, explore different career options, and join in discussions related to any field that interests you.

whom they might have worked with in the past. When using LinkedIn, always be mindful of the little things that still matter, such as having a professional email address rather than one that uses slang or personal nicknames.

While LinkedIn is considered one of the more accessible social media sites, it still has its own issues, two of them relating to contrast and operating the keyboard. *SociaBility: Social Media for People with a Disability* by Media Access Australia suggests ways to overcome and navigate these issues by offering tips on how to connect with other LinkedIn users if one can't see the photographs.

Chapter Five

Joining Forces with Allies

Facing the future as a disabled teen can be a frightening concept. But knowing that our allies, whether they be friends, parents, siblings, or health care providers, surround us and are ready and willing to offer support can make the journey much easier. The transition from adolescence to adulthood, particularly for those with disabilities, is complex. That's why it's critical to lean on one's allies for guidance.

A Smooth Transition

A transition marks the end of one known structure and routine and paves the way for a new one. When talking about transition for someone with a disability, it includes the possible move from school to work; living at home to living on one's own; and going from pediatric to adult health care teams. Switching health care teams can arguably be one of the more important parts of the transition process because everyone involved wants to make sure that a teen with a disability will be getting the

How to Advocate for Yourself

- Know what you might need: If you know what accommodations you need (for example, an accessible and ADA-compliant shower), your college or university can get that in place for you.
- Use resources early on: The college experience can be overwhelming at first, but there are many mechanisms in place to help students with disabilities succeed. Get in touch with your school's disability services office to get the ball rolling.
- Be assertive: Advocating for yourself is not an easy task. You may encounter another person who is difficult or doesn't know how to properly assist someone with a disability, if they even know that such assistance is needed. Taking control of your life and exhibiting confidence is vital.

best medical care possible. There are many health care providers—doctors, nurses, social workers, and physical and occupational therapists—who specialize in the transition to adulthood for adolescents with disabilities, an issue that is especially relevant when building and sustaining whatever networks they have formed.

Different Elements

There are many different elements involved in transition, many of which families may be unprepared to handle. In *On Your Own Without a Net: The Transition to Adulthood for Vulnerable Populations*, authors of sections of the book Robert Wm. Blum, Patience Haydock White, and Leslie Gallay, discuss how the journey of transition is made up of four major parts: 1) preparing early on for the transition to an adult system; 2) building skills in

College can be tough to navigate as a student with a disability, but with the right resources and a strong support network, you can succeed.

communication, decision making, assertiveness, and self-care; 3) moving on from school to the workforce; and finally, 4) independence.

The authors state that the transition for adolescents with disabilities should be a process, not just one event. It should ideally involve the youth's entire family as a support network. This process must be planned and must take into account the youth's age and the status of his or her medical condition and disability.

The transition process should begin at the time of diagnosis of the medical condition or disability and should include goals of achieving maximum independence and self-management. Late adolescence and early adulthood is the time when society expects an individual to begin making his or her own decisions about care and life in general.

In addition, a teen's doctors and health care team, including his or her family, must appreciate the transition and see it as a change in support, rather than a loss of support. Socially and emotionally, situations evolve, and the care a teen receives should evolve with it. For example, navigating college is a new circumstance that comes with its own set of entanglements and opportunities to thrive. What needs to be put in place in order for the teen to succeed in college academically, socially, and emotionally? How will she physically navigate? How will he stay connected to others in his network? It is imperative that a teen leaving the comfort of her home, where she has her parents to guide her knows all about self-advocacy. She must know how to stand up for herself and get what she needs to succeed.

An important part of a successful transition is having the disabled teen work alongside his health care providers, family, and allies to make sure that the teenager is readily prepared for his future. According to the IWD's website, the transition services they provide help women and teenage girls with disabilities explore ways to focus on health and wellness through fitness and creative expression; put together a health plan; meet other disabled teens with the goal of life-long friendships; share the trials and triumphs of living with a disability; and become educated

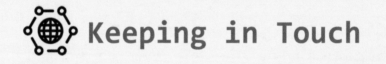 Keeping in Touch

It's important to stay in touch with your network when you're away at school. Some ways to do that include:

- Skype or FaceTime. Both of these applications are great ways to stay in close contact with parents, friends, mentors, or a significant other. Being able to see the other person's

(continued on the next page)

(continued from the previous page)

face and expressions may help the two of you feel more connected.

- Phone calls. Phone calls are preferable to texting because you can get a greater sense of what the other person is thinking or feeling when you hear the intonation in his voice. This can lead to more in-depth, productive conversations.
- Writing letters. Writing letters is a personal, heartfelt gesture. It's a wonderful feeling to receive letters in the mail from loved ones, as it shows that that person cares about and misses the person who has moved away to begin an adult life.

about resources for the disabled in their local communities. All of these elements are crucial because they touch on every aspect of how a transition may affect one's daily life.

Networking is an interesting and effective way to put yourself out there when trying to make connections in both your work and personal life. It is a useful marketing tool and offers disabled teens the chance to reflect on the ways in which their disability affects how they interact with others.

Having a disability should not prevent you from living a meaningful, fulfilling life. It may make certain situations more difficult, but that shouldn't stop

Although there are challenges that come with having a disability, these difficulties should not keep you from living a life filled with purpose and happiness. A supportive network of friends and allies will help you meet both your personal and professional goals.

you from achieving your goals. It's important to take the time to educate allies about your disability so they do not make assumptions based on stereotypes and can truly get to know you. If you have a strong support system in place, effective coping skills, and a positive attitude toward life, anything is possible.

10 Great Questions to Ask Your Pediatrician

1. How will the transition to adulthood affect the medical care I receive?

2. What are some coping skills I can use to deal with any anxiety around this transition?

3. Will you still be available as a resource after I transition?

4. How can I best advocate for myself during this time?

5. Can you recommended doctors to manage my care going forward?

6. Will you meet with those doctors to go over my case?

7. Who will handle my care if there is a lapse in time before my first appointment with the new doctor?

8. Will you include my support system in everything related to my continued care?

9. How will you keep my medical records confidential?

10. Can you point me to resources to help with the transition to college or employment?

Glossary

accessibility Whether something is able to be used, entered, seen, heard, or understood.

ADA-compliant Describing an object or place that follows the guidelines set forth by the Americans with Disabilities Act (ADA).

advocate A person who supports and defends someone else's cause.

ally A person who supports someone else, often those who are in a marginalized group.

blogging Writing on a website to share personal thoughts, opinions, or commentary about a particular topic.

cerebral palsy A neurological condition that affects muscle coordination and posture.

cyberbullying The use of social media to send harmful messages to bully, intimidate, or threaten another person.

disability A chronic condition or impairment that results in an inability to carry out daily activities.

health care provider A licensed professional who gives medical care.

holistic Based on a belief that the way to wellness is through interconnectedness and a focus on a person's medical and emotional life.

independence The state of being self-sufficient or free from outside control.

muscular dystrophy A medical condition in which a person's muscles weaken over time.

network A group of people who offer one

another support and information in service of a common purpose.

pediatrician A medical doctor who specializes in treating children and adolescents.

self-advocacy The act of representing oneself in order to secure the support and resources needed to be successful.

social media A platform used to communicate with other users and to share information and develop an online social network.

stigma A set of negative beliefs about a specific part of someone's identity.

transition The process of moving from one state of being to another. In this resource, refers to a disabled teen moving forward to adulthood.

wellness The path toward reaching one's full potential and a state of positive mental, emotional, and spiritual health.

For More Information

American Association of People with Disabilities (AAPD)
2013 H Street NW
Washington, DC 20006
(202) 521-4316
Website: https://www.aapd.com
Facebook: @DisabilityPowered
Twitter: @AAPD
AAPD advocates for people with disabilities in the areas of education, independent living, and access to assistive technology.

Camp SMILE
c/o United Cerebral Palsy Mobile
3058 Dolphin Square Connector
Mobile, AL 36607
Website: http://www.campsmilemobile.org
Facebook: @UCPCampSMILE
Camp SMILE is a summer camp for people with disabilities that is sponsored by United Cerebral Palsy.

Canadian Foundation for Physically Disabled Persons (CFPDP)
6 Garamound Court, Suite 265
Toronto, ON M3C 175
Canada
Website: https://www.cfpdp.com
Facebook and Twitter: @cffpdp
This foundation's goals include raising awareness

about the issues that people with disabilities face as well as their achievements. They also present conferences, seminars, and meetings to support the disabled.

Disability Allies
Young Adult Community Inclusion Center
415 Route 18 South
East Brunswick, NJ 08816
(908) 616-5091
Website: https://www.disabilityallies.com
Twitter: @DisAllies
Instagram: @disallies
Disability Allies mission is to facilitate friendships between young adults and teens with and without disabilities.

Initiative for Women with Disabilities (IWD)
359 Second Avenue
New York, NY 10010
(212) 598-6429
Website: https://nyulangone.org/locations /initiative-for-women-with-disabilities
Facebook: @Initiativeforwomenwithdisabilities
IWD operates under NYU Langone Health and provides primary and gynecological care for women with disabilities as well as wellness services, fitness classes, and adaptive sports programs.

PACE
970 Lawrence Avenue W, #210
North York, ON M6A 3B6
Canada

(416) 789-7806
Email: pace@pace-il.ca
Website: http://www.pace-il.ca
PACE is a nonprofit community organization that
provides support services to adults with disabilities so they may live full lives, with as much
independence as their condition allows. PACE
also offers supportive housing, which allows res-
idents to live on their own with the help of highly
trained staff.

United Cerebral Palsy (UCP)
1825 K Street NW, Suite 600
Washington, DC 200006
(800) 872-5827
Website: http://ucp.org
Facebook: @unitedcerebralpalsy
Twitter: @UCPnational
UCP offers educational, advocacy, and direct
support services to people with a range
of disabilities.

For Further Reading

Barnard, Sara. *A Quiet Kind of Thunder.* London, UK: Macmillan Children's Books, 2017.

Lowry, Lois. *Gathering Blue.* New York, NY: Harper-Collins Children's Books, 2014.

Paddock, Bonner. *One More Step: My Story of Living with Cerebral Palsy, Climbing Kilimanjaro, and Surviving the Hardest Race on Earth.* New York, NY: HarperOne, 2015.

Palacio, R. J. *Wonder.* New York, NY: Knopf, 2017.

Phillbrick, Rodman. *Freak the Mighty.* 20th anniversary edition. New York, NY: Blue Sky Press, 2013.

Reyl, Hilary. *Kids Like Us.* New York, NY: Farrar, Straus, and Giroux, 2017.

Stefonek, Jeannie. *Act It Out! One Year of Social Skills Lessons for Students Grades 7–12.* Lenexa, KS: AAPC Publishing, 2016.

Sundquist, Josh. *Love and First Sight.* Boston, MA: Little, Brown Books for Young Readers, 2018.

Thomas, Leah. *Nowhere Near You.* New York, NY: Bloomsbury, 2017.

Wolk, Laurie. *Girls Just Want to Have Likes: How to Raise Confident Girls in the Face of Social Media Madness*. New York, NY: Morgan James Publishing, 2017.

Bibliography

Amado, A. N. *Friends: Connecting People with Disabilities and Community Members*. Minneapolis, MN: University of Minnesota, 2013.

Carter, Erik, Jennifer Asmus, and Colleen Moss. "Fostering Friendships: Supporting Relationships among Youth with and without Developmental Disabilities." *Prevention Researcher* 20, no. 2, 2013.

Corbitt, Anna. "How to Be an Ally of the Disability Community." Paraquad: The Disability Experts, July 21, 2016. https://www.paraquad.org/blog/how-to-be-an-ally-of-the-disability-community.

Disability Allies. "Disability Allies: Our Mission." Retrieved March 5, 2018. https://www.disabilityallies.com/about-us.

Diversability. "Teen Girls with Disabilities Get to Writing: Learn about Girl Fuse." May 19, 2016. http://www.mydiversability.com/blog/2016/5/19/teen-girls-with-disabilities-get-to-writing-learn-about-the-new-disability-initiative-from-teen-voices.

Freleng, Maggie. "For Teens with Disabilities, Flirting Can Be Easier Online." Huffington Post, June 12, 2013. https://www.huffingtonpost.com/2013/06/12/disabled-teens-online-dating_n_3430249.html.

Gerhardt, S. "The Goal of Making Friends for Youth with Disabilities: Creating a Goal Menu." *Child : Care, Health & Development* 41, no. 6 (November 1, 2015).

Hettler, Bill. "The Six Dimensions of Wellness." National Wellness Institute. Retrieved January 15, 2018. http://www.nationalwellness .org/?page=six_dimensions.

Jackson, Linda. "How a Project for Disabled Teenagers Is Changing Lives." *The Guardian*, March 19, 2015. https://www.theguardian.com/social-care -network/2015/mar/19/cornish-project -disability-young-people.

Kraus, Lewis. *2016 Disability Statistics Annual Report*. Durham, NH: University of New Hampshire, 2017.

Lu, Wendy. "Dating with a Disability." *New York Times*, December 8, 2016. https://www.nytimes .com/2016/12/08/well/family/dating-with-a -disability.html.

Media Access Australia. "Sociability: Social Media for People with a Disability." 2011. https:// mediaaccess.org.au/web/social-media -for-people-with-a-disability.

StopBullying.gov. "Prevent Cyberbullying: Be Aware of What Your Kids Are Doing Online." Retrieved February 19, 2018. https://www.stopbullying .gov/cyberbullying/prevention/index.html.

Women's E-News. "Girl Fuse." Retrieved January 29, 2018. https://womensenews.org/teen-voices /girl-fuse.

Index

About the Author

Marcela D. Grillo has cerebral palsy and a strong passion and love for writing, advocating, and educating others about what it means to live with a disability. She has lived the struggles and successes of being a disabled young woman in today's able-bodied society. In the summer of 2015, Grillo helped develop a comprehensive lecture series for youth and adolescents with cerebral palsy transitioning to adulthood at NYU Langone Hospital for Joint Diseases. Grillo received her BA in English literature from Connecticut College and is currently completing a premedical certificate at Columbia University as she prepares to pursue a medical degree.

Photo Credits

Cover, p. 1 Lokibaho/E+/Getty Images; p. 5 Brian Mitchell/Corbis Documentary/Getty Images; p. 6 LJM Photo/Design Pics/Getty Images; p. 9 Aelitta/iStock/Thinkstock; p. 10 Silverkblackstock/Shutterstock.com; p. 11 Mikos/iStock/Thinkstock; p. 16 Pacific Press/LightRocket/Getty Images; p. 18 Michaelpuche/iStock/Thinkstock; p. 20 NurPhoto/Getty Images; p. 21 Monkey Business Images/Shutterstock.com; p. 24 Bloomberg/Getty Images; p. 25 Blend Images/Alamy Stock Photo; p. 28 Daisy Daisy/Shutterstock.com; p. 30 Jose Luis Pelaez/Photodisc/Getty Images; p. 34 Mark J Hunt/Getty Images; p. 35 © AP Images; p. 38 © iStockphoto.com/kali9; p. 43 S3studio/Getty Images; p. 47 Skynesher/E+/Getty Images; p. 51 Graham Oliver/Juice Images/Getty Images.

Design: Tahara Anderson; Editor: Jennifer Landau; Photo Researcher: Sherri Jackson